PIANO | VOCAL | GUITAR • CD   **VOLUME 46**

HAL•LEONARD®

PIANO PLAY-ALONG

AUDIO ACCESS INCLUDED

A NEW MUSICAL
WICKED

MUSIC & LYRICS BY STEPHEN SCHWARTZ

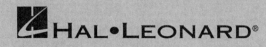

T0083951

PLAYBACK+
Speed • Pitch • Balance • Loop

To access audio, visit:
www.halleonard.com/mylibrary

Enter Code
5906-6921-3013-4065

ISBN 978-1-4234-1108-6

HAL•LEONARD®

Visit Hal Leonard Online at
www.halleonard.com

Contact Us:
Hal Leonard
7777 West Bluemound Road
Milwaukee, WI 53213
Email: info@halleonard.com

In Europe contact:
Hal Leonard Europe Limited
Distribution Centre, Newmarket Road
Bury St Edmunds, Suffolk, IP33 3YB
Email: info@halleonardeurope.com

In Australia contact:
Hal Leonard Australia Pty. Ltd.
4 Lentara Court
Cheltenham, Victoria, 3192 Australia
Email: info@halleonard.com.au

CONTENTS

PAGE TITLE

DANCING THROUGH LIFE

Music and Lyrics by
STEPHEN SCHWARTZ

Freely

FIYERO:

The trou-ble with school is ____ they al-ways try to teach the wrong les-son. ____

Be-lieve me, I've been kicked out of e-nough of them ____ to know. ____

They

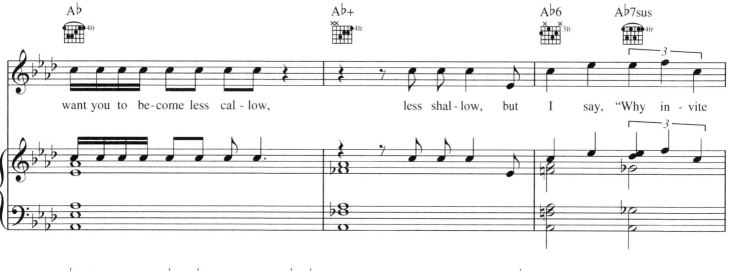

want you to be-come less cal-low, less shal-low, but I say, "Why in-vite

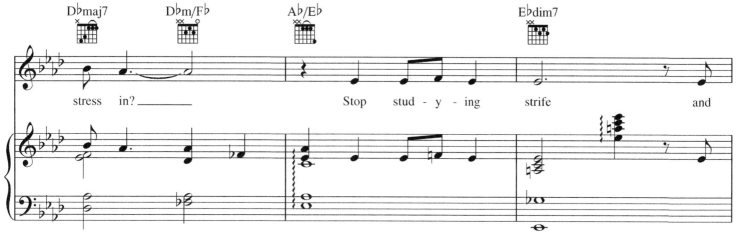

stress in? _____ Stop stud-y-ing strife and

Pop "Dance beat"

learn to live 'the un-ex-am-ined life' "... _____

mp legato

With pedal

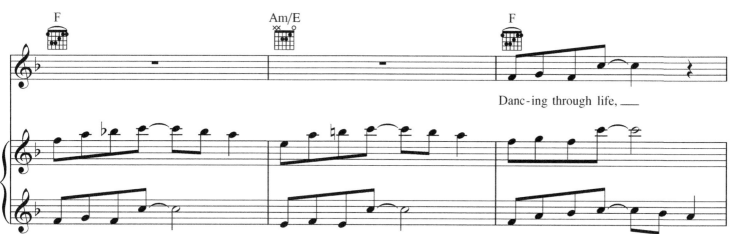

Danc-ing through life, ___

skim-ming the sur - face, glid-ing where turf ___ is smooth. ___

Life's more pain - less for the brain - less. Why think too hard ___

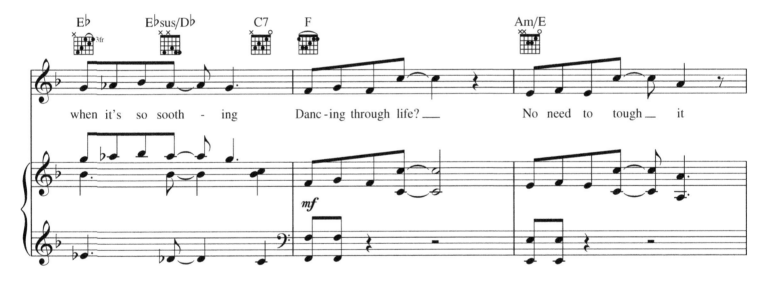

when it's so sooth - ing Danc-ing through life? ___ No need to tough ___ it

when you can slough ___ it off ___ as I do. ___ Noth-ing mat - ters, but

know-ing noth-ing mat-ters ___ It's just life so keep danc - ing

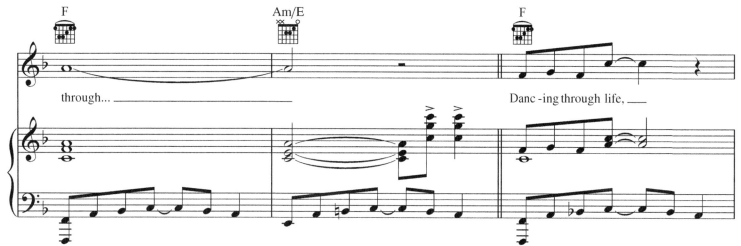

through... ___ Danc -ing through life, ___

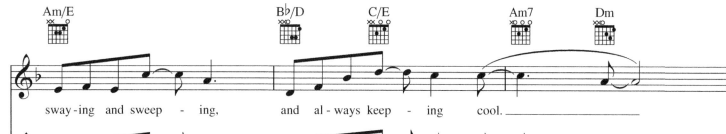

sway-ing and sweep - ing, and al - ways keep - ing cool. ___

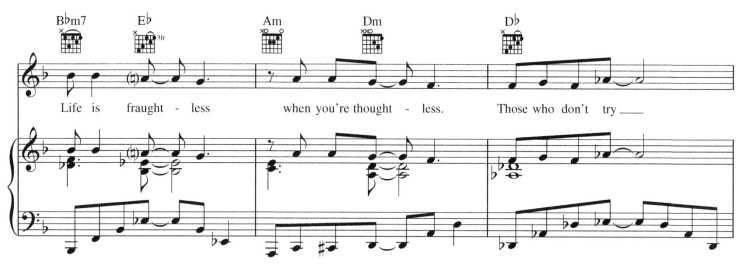

Life is fraught - less when you're thought - less. Those who don't try ___

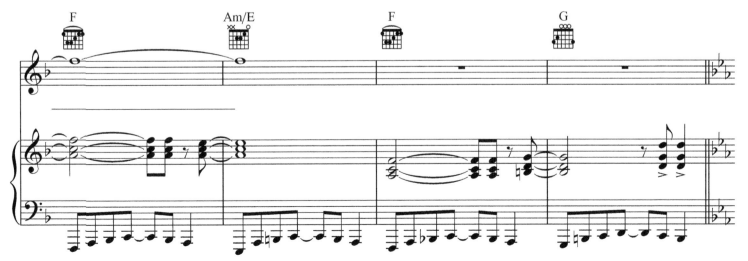

you'll be hap - py to be _____ there... _____

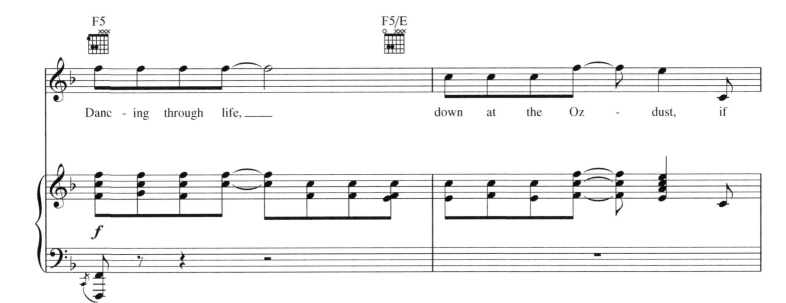

Danc - ing through life, _____ down at the Oz - dust, if

on - ly be - cause _____ dust is what we come to... _____ Noth - ing mat - ters but

know-ing noth-ing mat - ters, ___ It's just life ___

___ so keep danc - ing through. ___

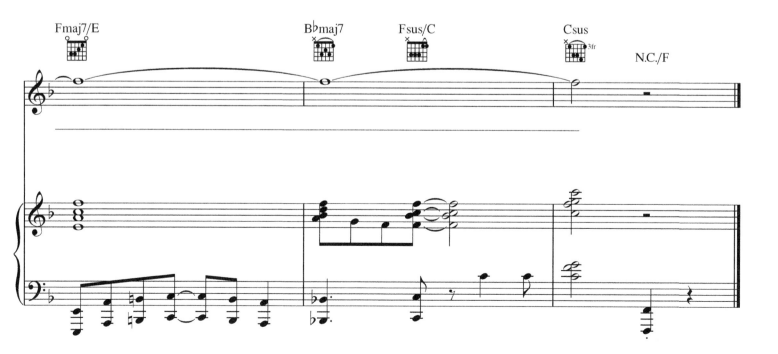

DEFYING GRAVITY

Music and Lyrics by
STEPHEN SCHWARTZ

Freely, with quiet intensity

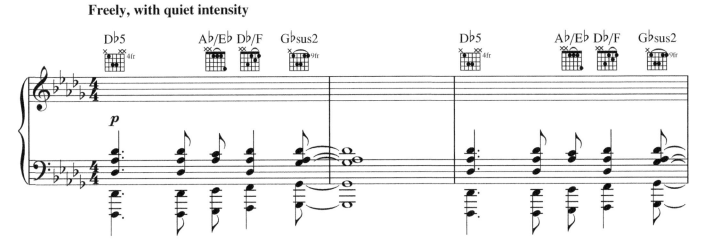

ELPHABA:

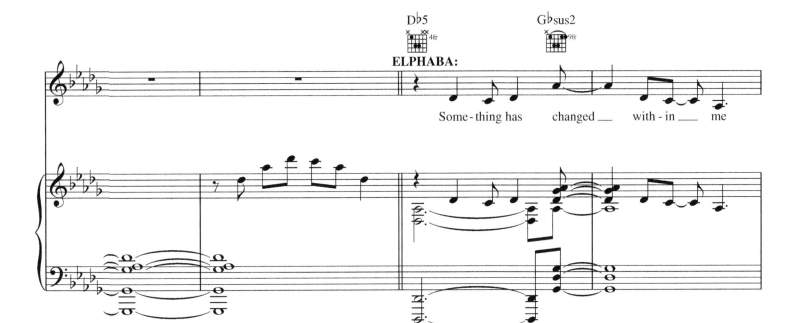

Some-thing has changed ____ with-in ____ me

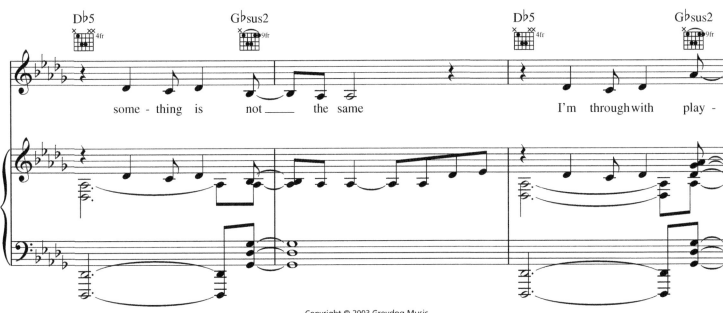

some - thing is not ____ the same   I'm through with play -

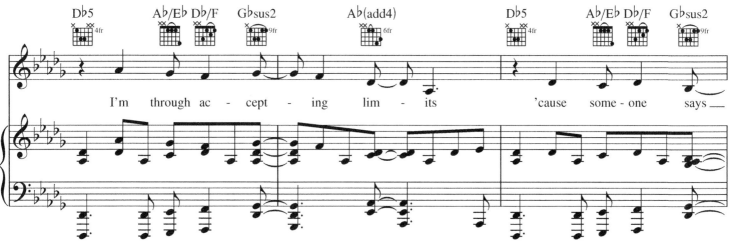

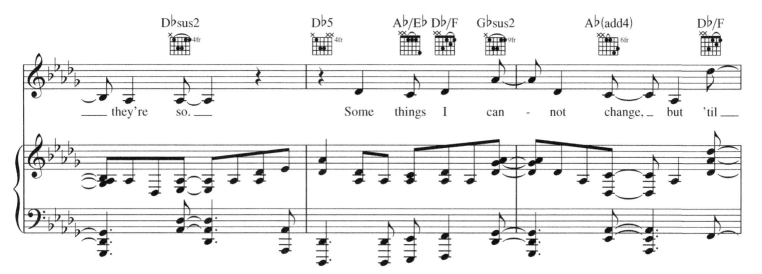

I'm through ac - cept - ing lim - its 'cause some - one says ___

___ they're so. ___ Some things I can - not change, _ but 'til ___

I try, ___ I'll nev - er know ___ Too long I've been ___

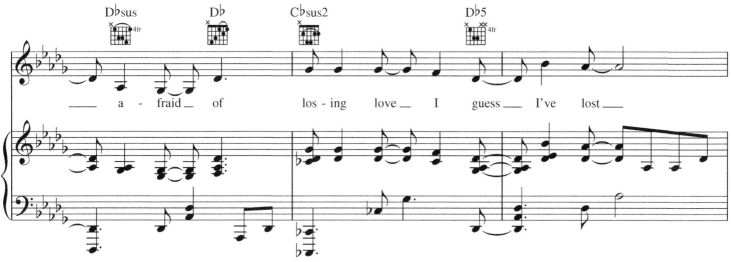

___ a - fraid _ of los - ing love _ I guess ___ I've lost ___

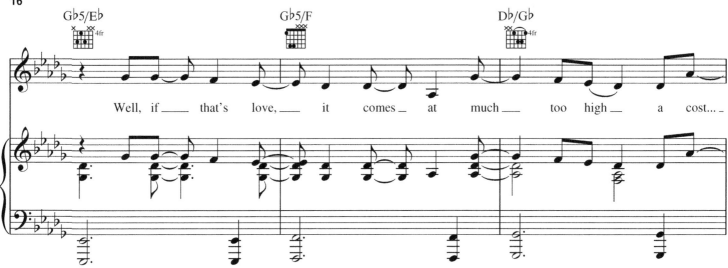

Well, if ____ that's love, ____ it comes ____ at much ____ too high ____ a cost... ____

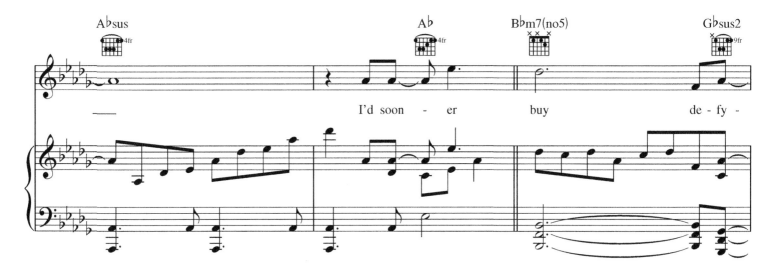

____ I'd soon - er buy de - fy -

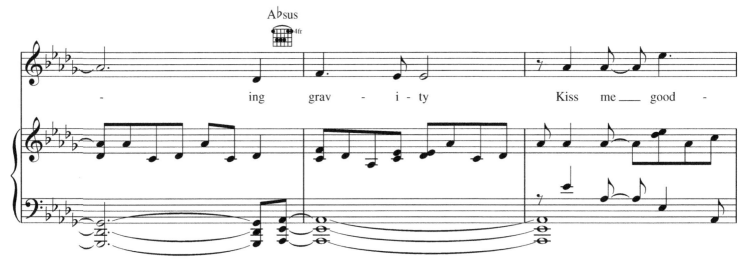

- ing grav - i - ty Kiss me ____ good -

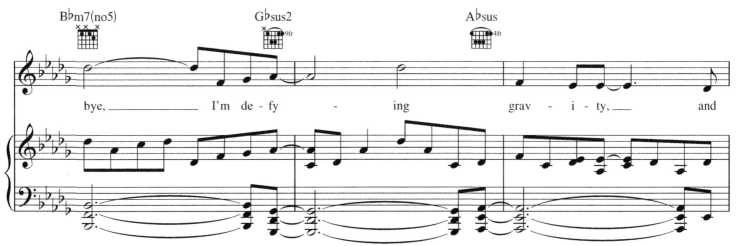

bye, ____ I'm de - fy - ing grav - i - ty, ____ and

Moderato, dreamily

you can't pull __ me down. _____

Un - lim - it - ed... _____ My fu - ture is

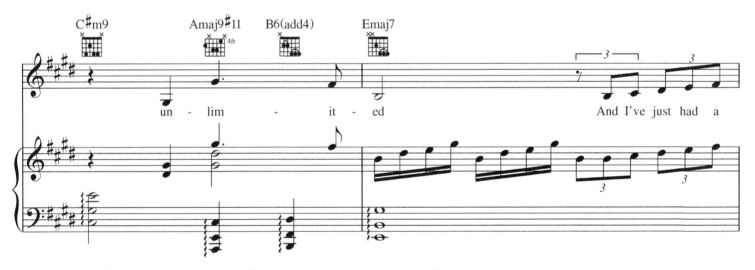

un - lim - it - ed And I've just had a

vi - sion al - most like a proph - e - cy, I know—

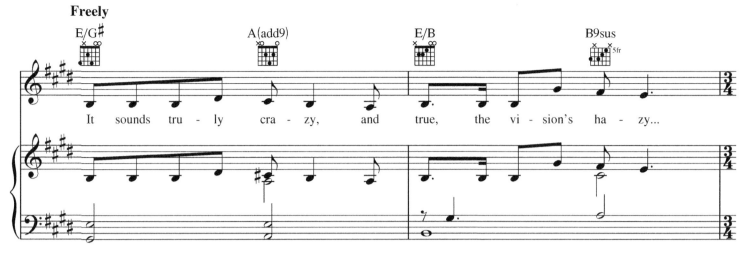

It sounds tru - ly cra - zy, and true, the vi - sion's ha - zy...

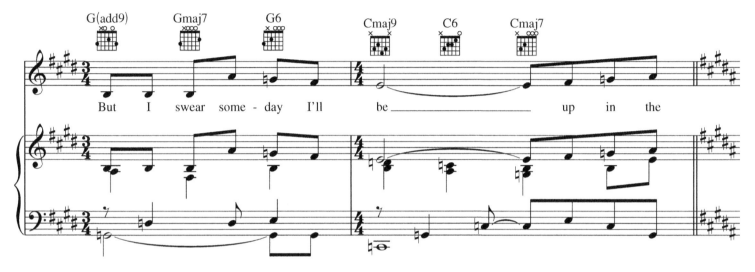

But I swear some - day I'll be _____ up in the

Allegro; as before

sky, de - fy - ing grav - i - ty

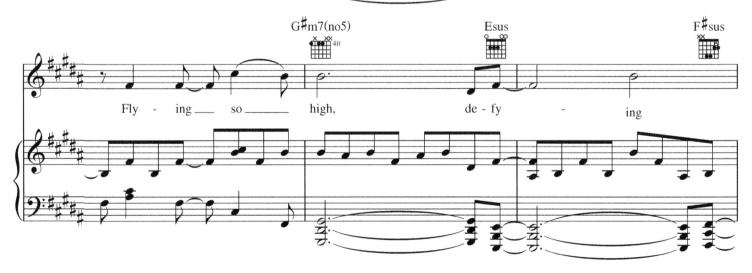

Fly - ing __ so __ high, de - fy - ing

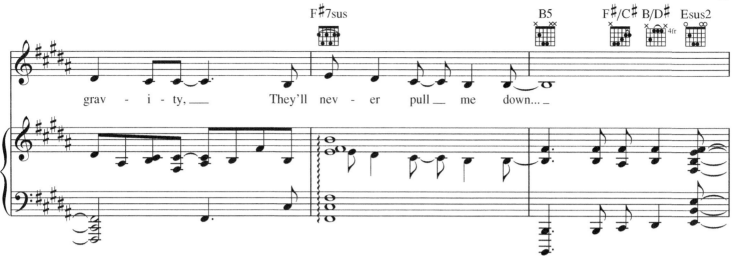

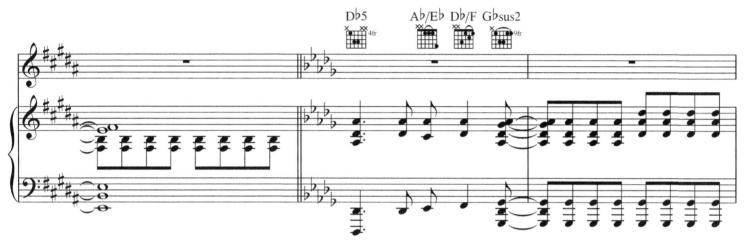

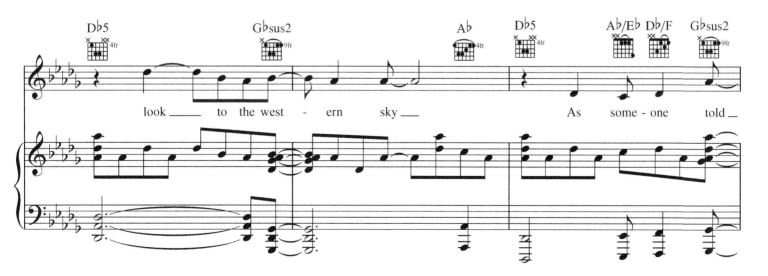

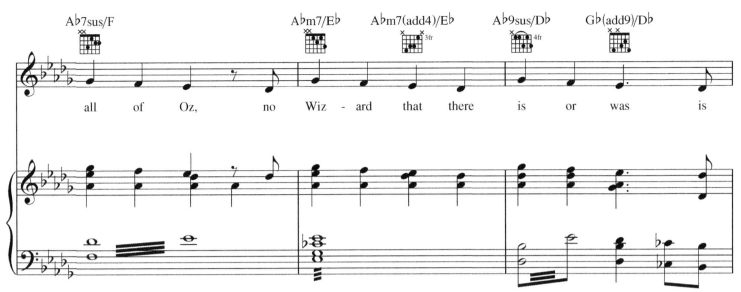

all of Oz, no Wiz - ard that there is or was is

ev - er gon - na bring me down... _____

_____ Ah!

FOR GOOD

Music and Lyrics by
STEPHEN SCHWARTZ

Note: When performed as a solo, sing the top melody line throughout.

Tenderly, poco rubato

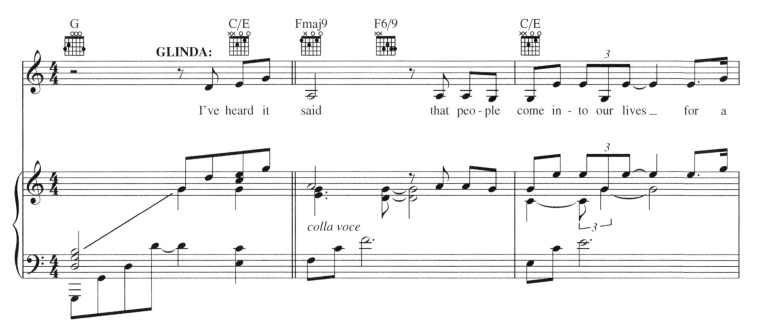

GLINDA:

I've heard it said that peo-ple come in-to our lives __ for a

colla voce

rea- son, bring-ing some-thing we must learn. And we are led to those who

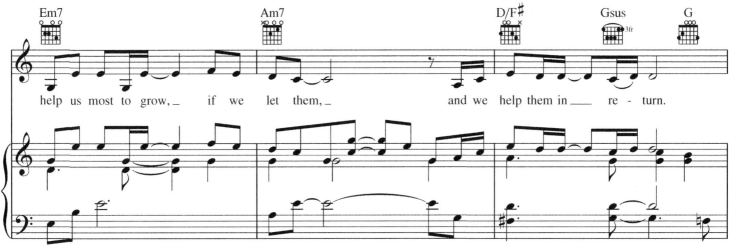

help us most to grow, _ if we let them, _ and we help them in __ re - turn.

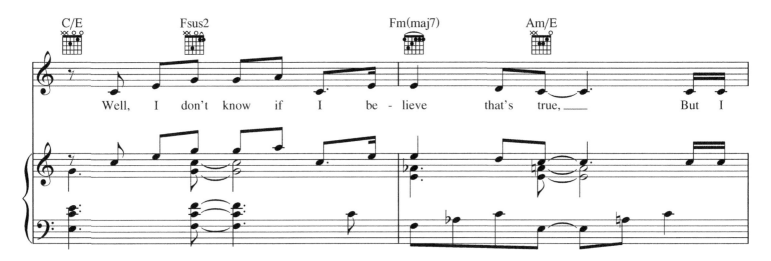

Well, I don't know if I be - lieve that's true, ___ But I

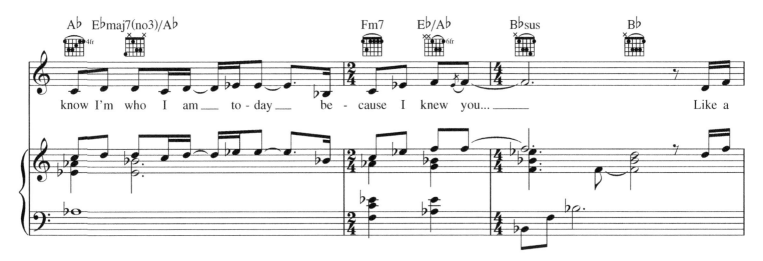

know I'm who I am __ to - day __ be - cause I knew you... ____ Like a

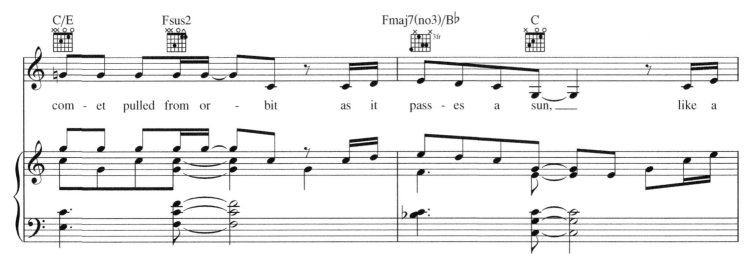

com - et pulled from or - bit as it pass - es a sun, ___ like a

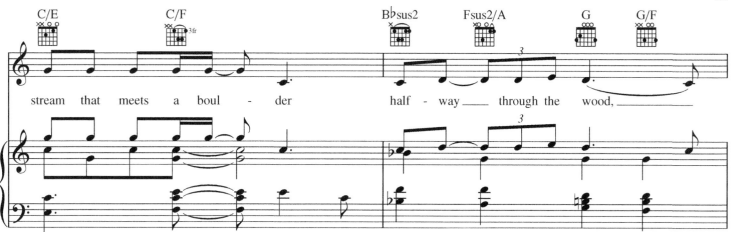

stream that meets a boul - der half - way ___ through the wood, ___

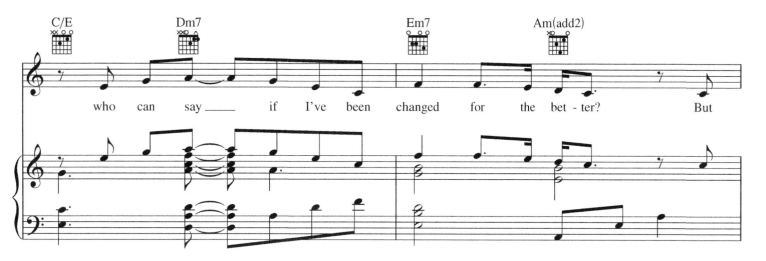

who can say ___ if I've been changed for the bet - ter? But

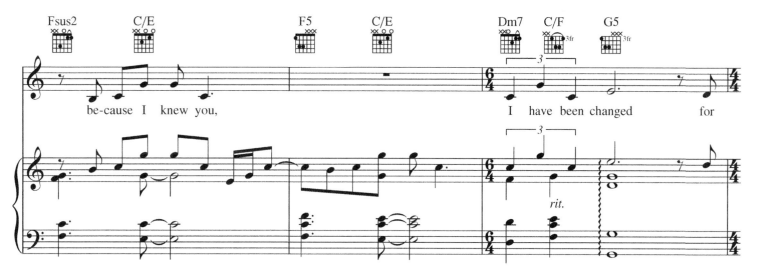

be-cause I knew you, I have been changed for

A tempo, warmly

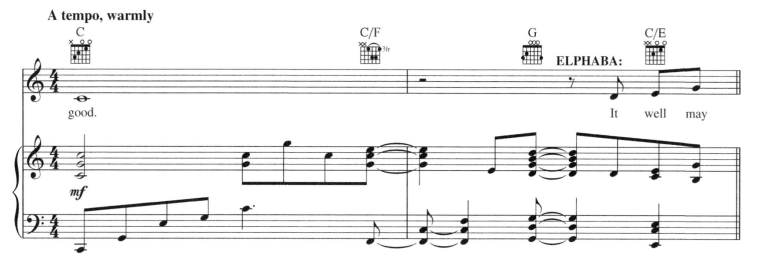

good. ELPHABA: It well may

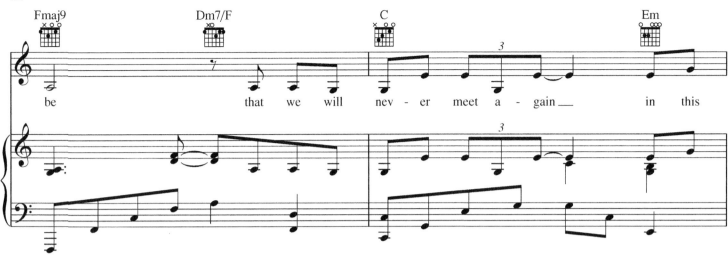

be that we will nev-er meet a-gain __ in this

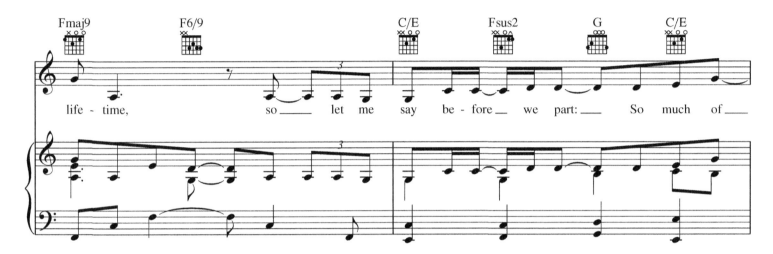

life - time, so __ let me say be-fore __ we part: __ So much of __

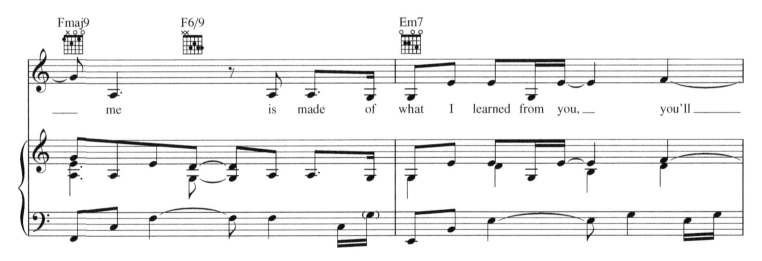

__ me is made of what I learned from you, __ you'll __

__ be with me __ like a hand-print on my __ heart.

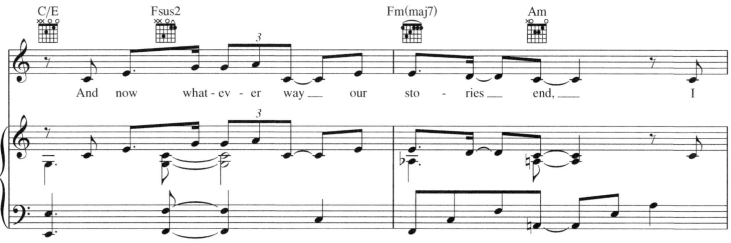

And now what-ev-er way ___ our sto-ries ___ end, ___ I

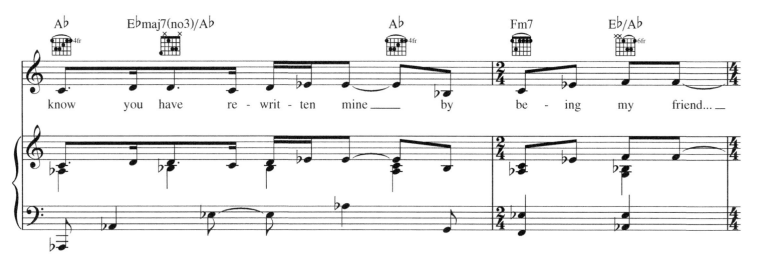

know you have re-writ-ten mine ___ by be-ing my friend... ___

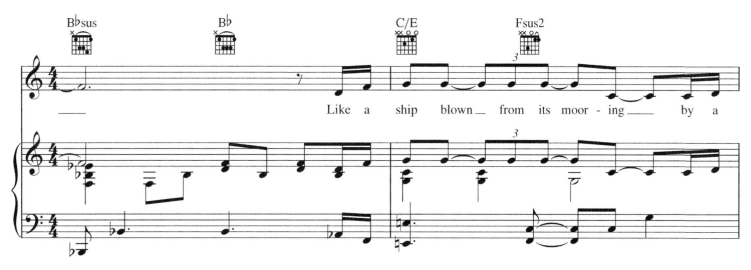

Like a ship blown ___ from its moor-ing ___ by a

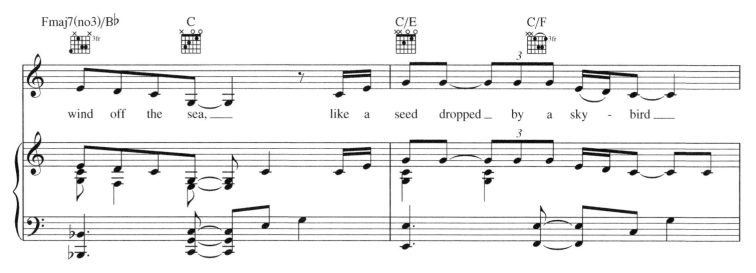

wind off the sea, ___ like a seed dropped ___ by a sky-bird ___

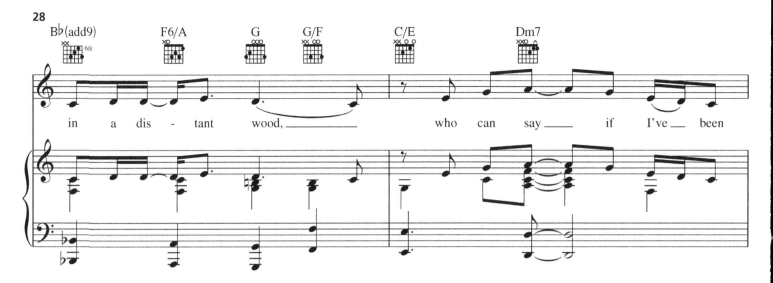

in a dis - tant wood, _____ who can say _____ if I've _____ been

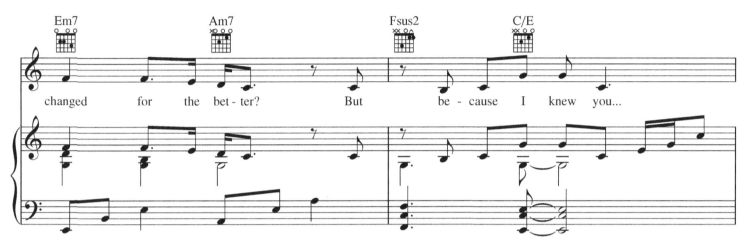

changed for the bet - ter? But be - cause I knew you...

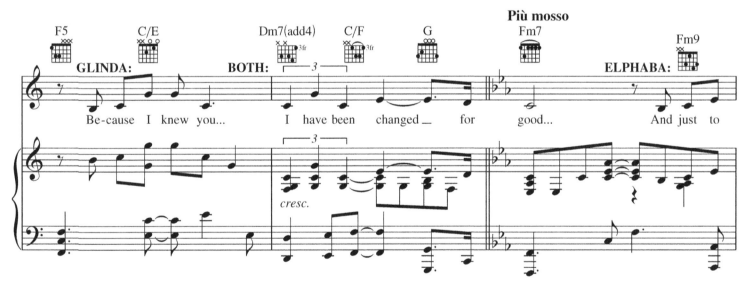

Più mosso

GLINDA: BOTH: Be-cause I knew you... I have been changed _____ for good... ELPHABA: And just to

clear the air, I ask for - give - ness for the things I've done _____ you

blame me ___ for. ___   **GLINDA:** But then, I guess _ we know there's

blame ___ to share, ___ and none of it seems to mat - ter an - y -

ELPHABA:

and none of it seems to mat - ter an - y -

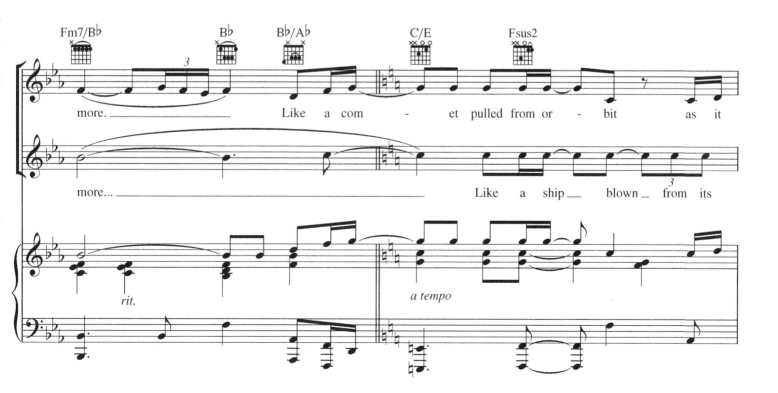

more. ___ Like a com - et pulled from or - bit as it

more... ___ Like a ship _ blown _ from its

rit.   *a tempo*

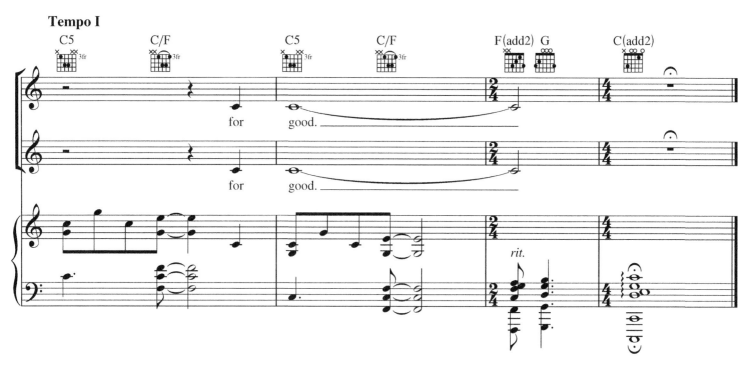

I COULDN'T BE HAPPIER

Music and Lyrics by
STEPHEN SCHWARTZ

Andante, melancholy

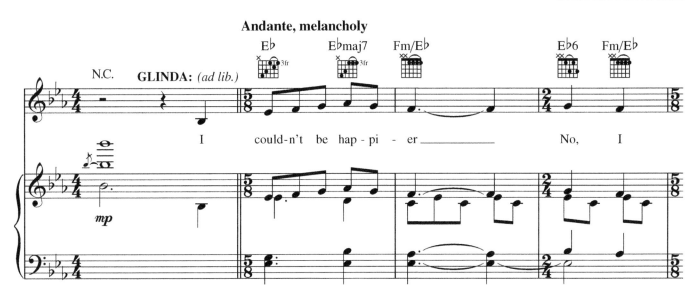

GLINDA: (ad lib.)

I could-n't be hap-pi-er _____ No, I

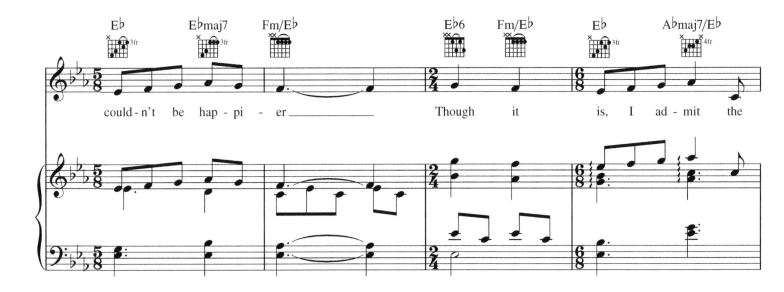

could-n't be hap-pi-er _____ Though it is, I ad-mit the

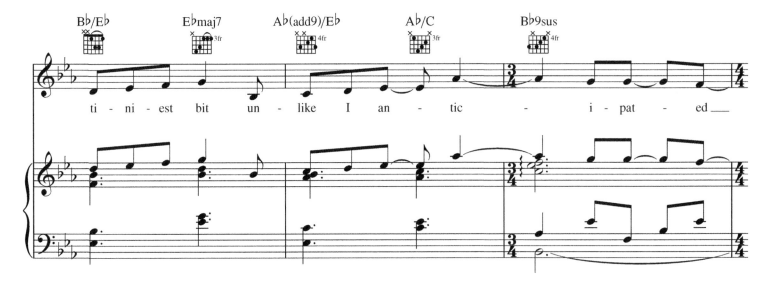

ti-ni-est bit un-like I an-tic-i-pat-ed _____

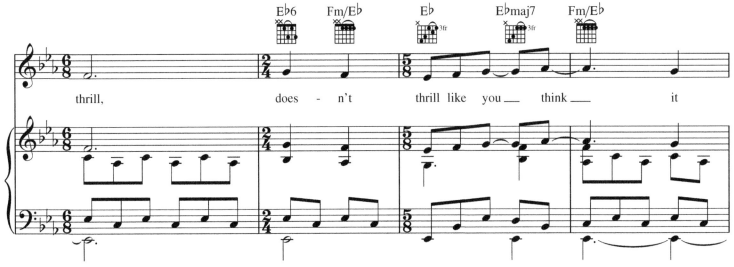

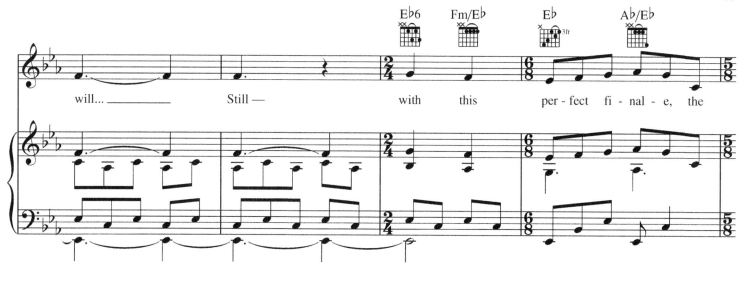

will... _____ Still — with this per - fect fi - nal - e, the

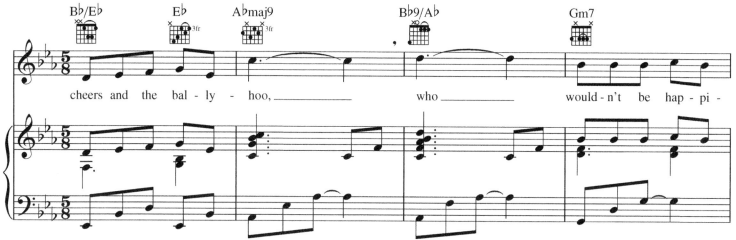

cheers and the bal - ly - hoo, _____ who _____ would - n't be hap - pi -

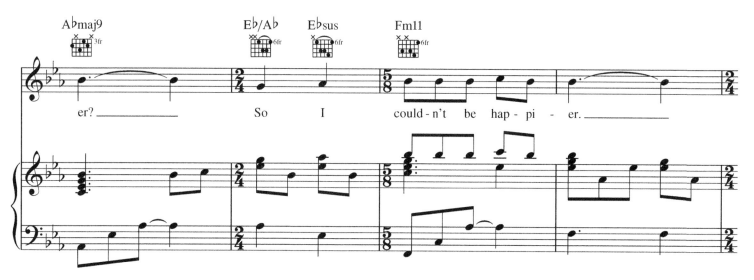

er? _____ So I could - n't be hap - pi - er. _____

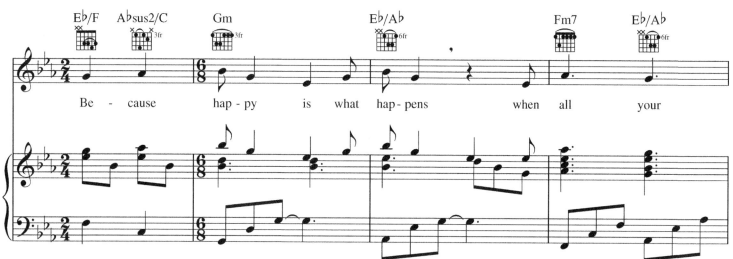

Be - cause hap - py is what hap - pens when all your

Reflectively

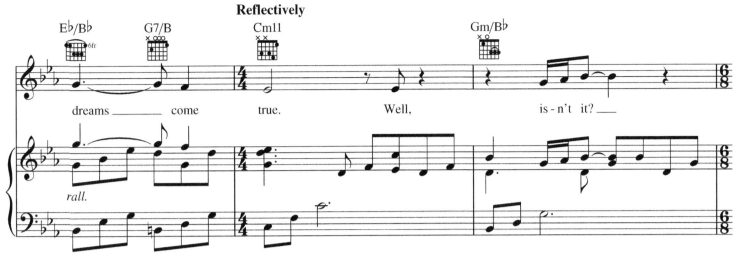

dreams _____ come true. Well, is - n't it? ____

rall.

A tempo, with forced joy

Hap - py is what hap - pens when your dreams _____

cresc.

opt.

come _____ true. ____

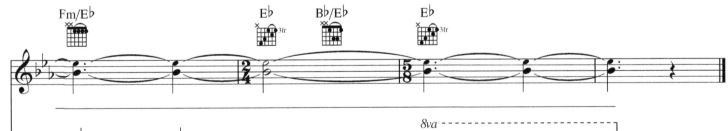

poco a poco rall.

I'M NOT THAT GIRL

Music and Lyrics by
STEPHEN SCHWARTZ

38

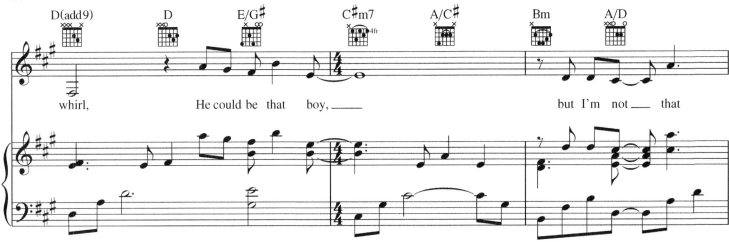

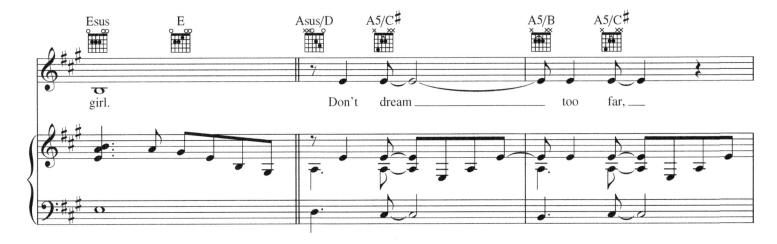

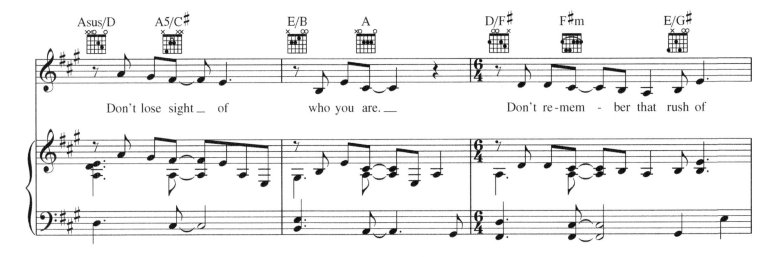

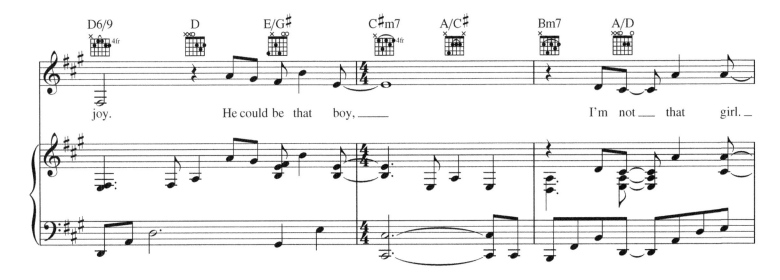

Ev - 'ry so of - ten we long to steal to the

land of What - Might - Have - Been, _____ But that does - n't soft - en the

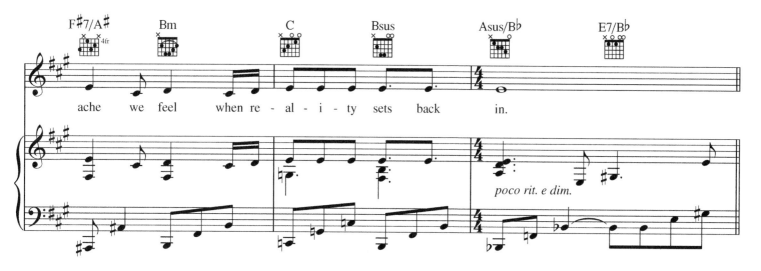

ache we feel when re - al - i - ty sets back in.

Tempo I

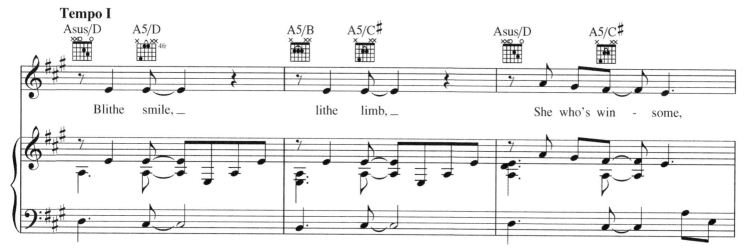

Blithe smile, _ lithe limb, _ She who's win - some,

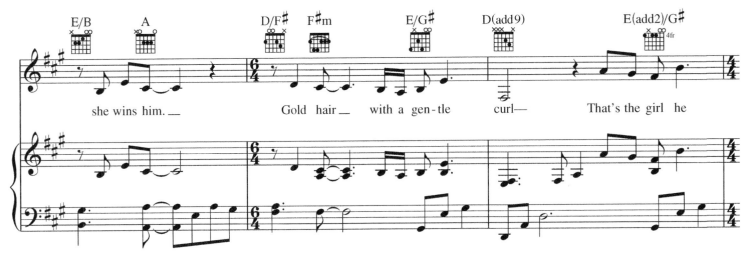

she wins him. ___ Gold hair ___ with a gen-tle curl— That's the girl he

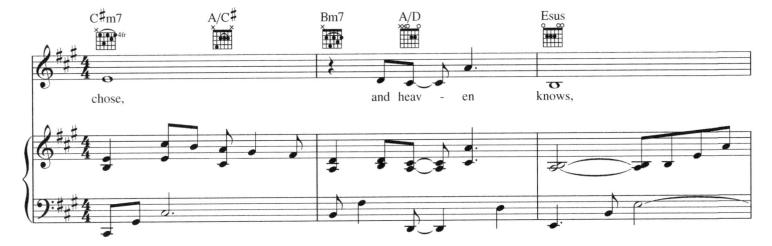

chose, and heav - en knows,

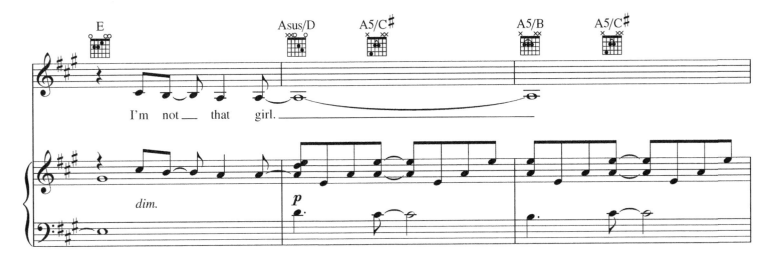

I'm not ___ that girl. ___

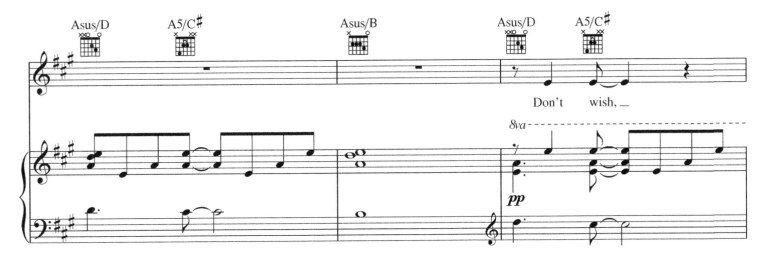

Don't wish, ___

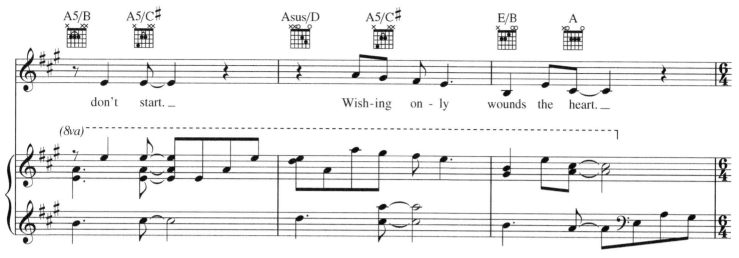

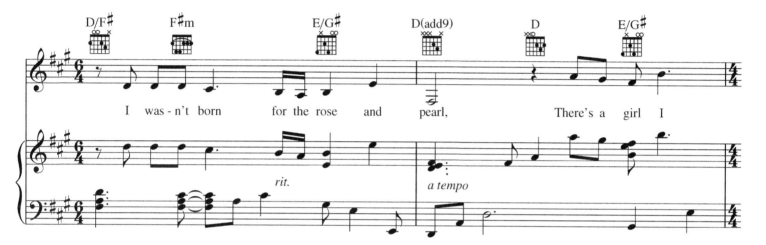

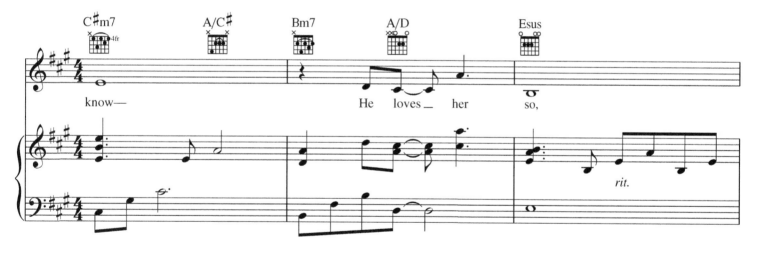

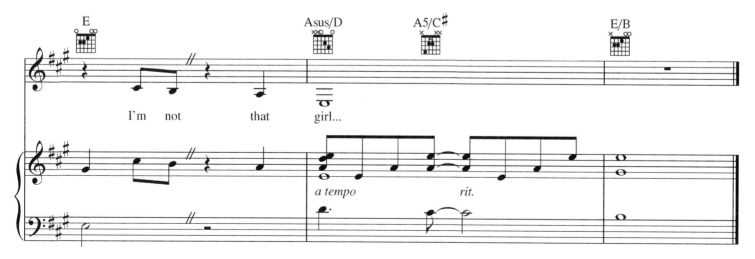

POPULAR

Music and Lyrics by
STEPHEN SCHWARTZ

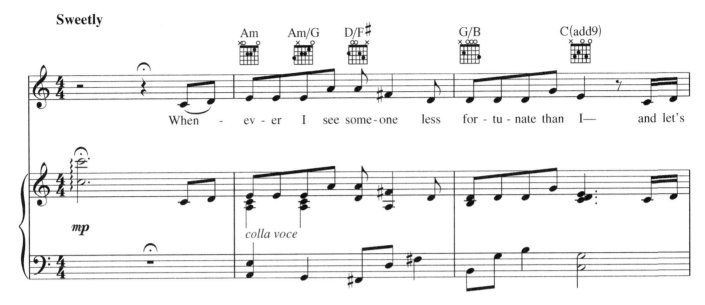

Sweetly

When-ev-er I see some-one less for-tu-nate than I— and let's

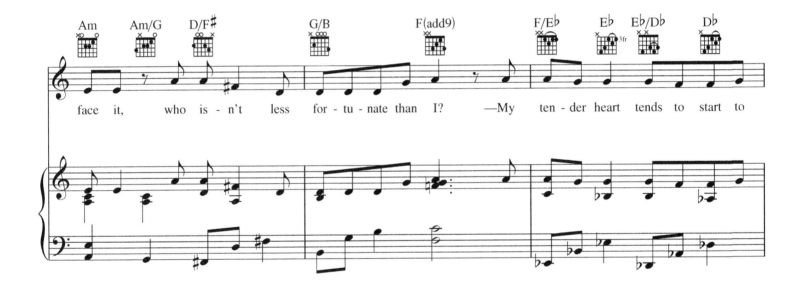

face it, who is-n't less for-tu-nate than I? —My ten-der heart tends to start to

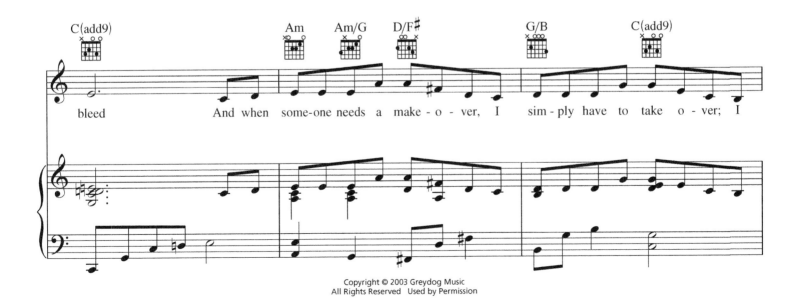

bleed And when some-one needs a make-o-ver, I sim-ply have to take o-ver; I

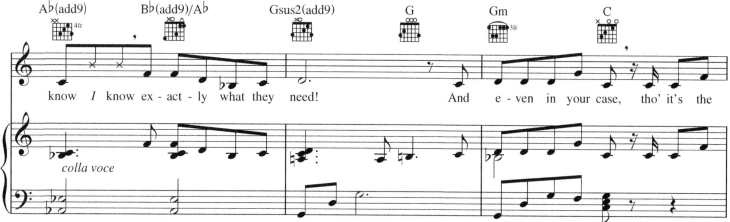

know _I_ know ex - act - ly what they need! And e - ven in your case, tho' it's the

colla voce

tough - est case I've yet to face,___ don't wor - ry, I'm de - ter - mined to suc -

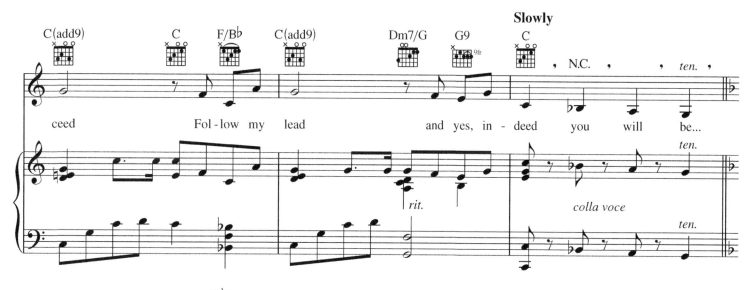

ceed Fol - low my lead and yes, in - deed you will be...

rit. *colla voce*

Bright and bubbly

Pop - u - lar,___ You're gon - na be pop - u - lar! I'll teach __ you the

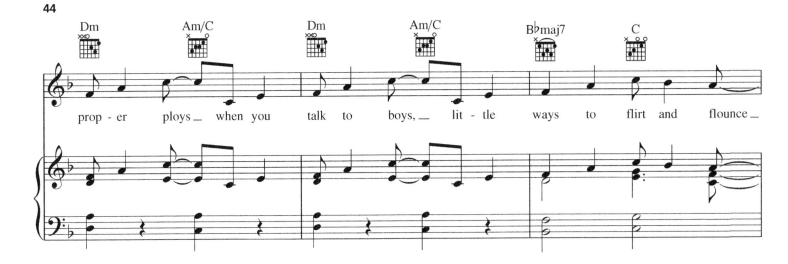

prop - er ploys __ when you talk to boys, __ lit - tle ways to flirt and flounce __

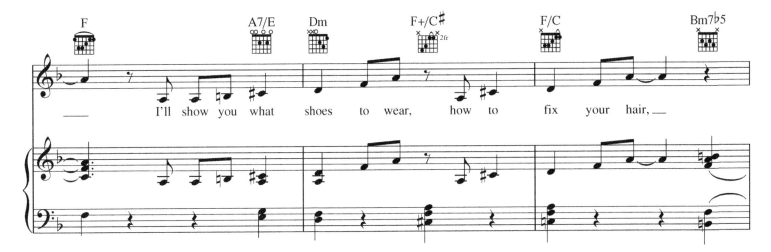

__ I'll show you what shoes to wear, how to fix your hair, __

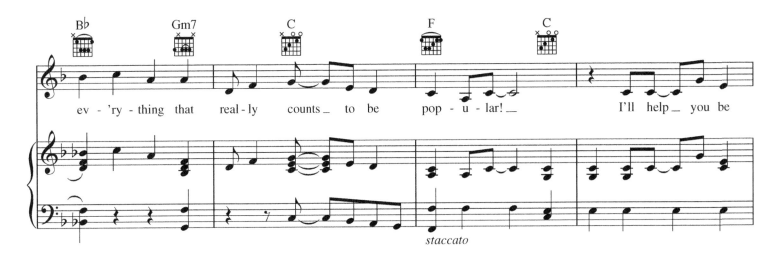

ev - 'ry - thing that real - ly counts __ to be pop - u - lar! __ I'll help __ you be

staccato

pop - u - lar! You'll hang __ with the right co - horts, __ you'll be

-ter and ad - vis - er, there's ___ no - bod - y wis - er, not ___ when it comes ___ to

pop - u - lar ___ I know ___ a - bout pop - u - lar!

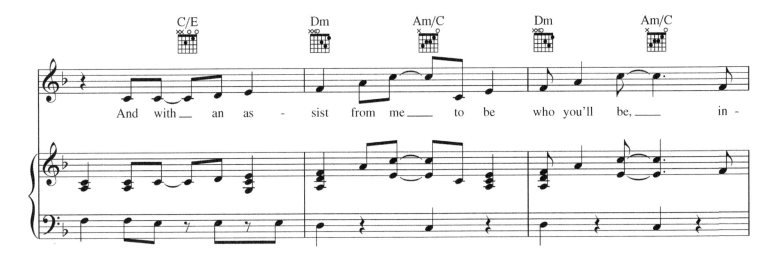

And with ___ an as - sist from me ___ to be who you'll be, ___ in-

stead of drear - y who - you - were... ___ are... There's noth - ing that can stop you from ___

be - com - ing pop - u - ler... lar... _____

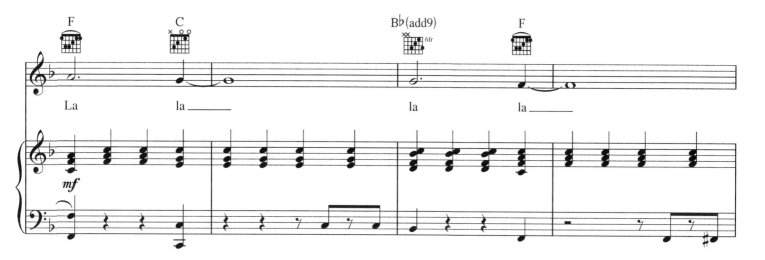

La la _____ la la _____

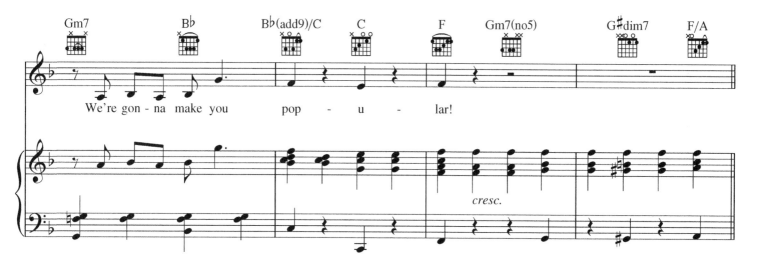

We're gon - na make you pop - u - lar!

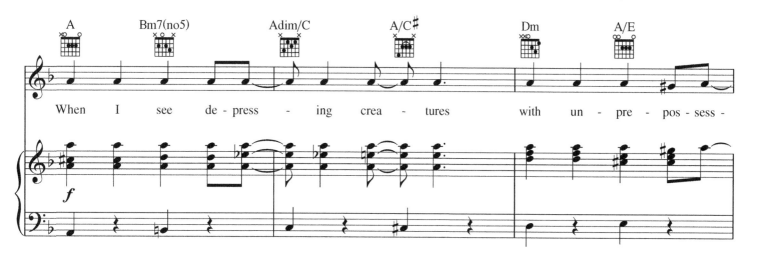

When I see de - press - ing crea - tures with un - pre - pos - sess -

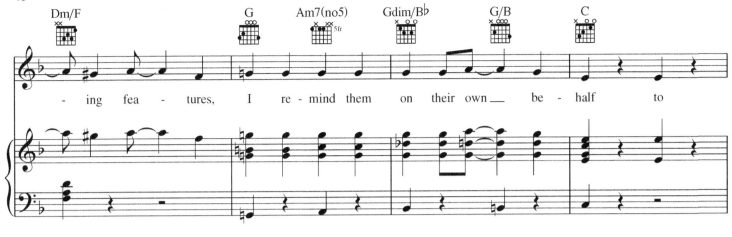

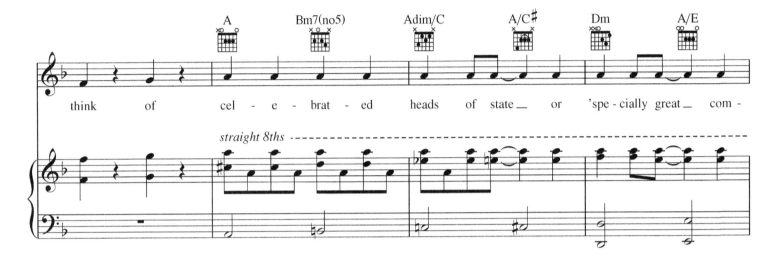

pop - u - lar! It's not __ a - bout ap - ti - tude, __ it's the

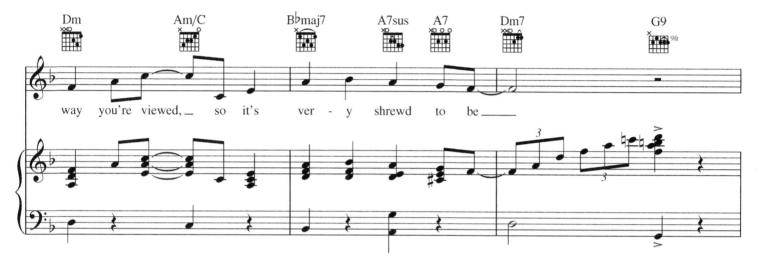

way you're viewed, __ so it's ver - y shrewd to be __

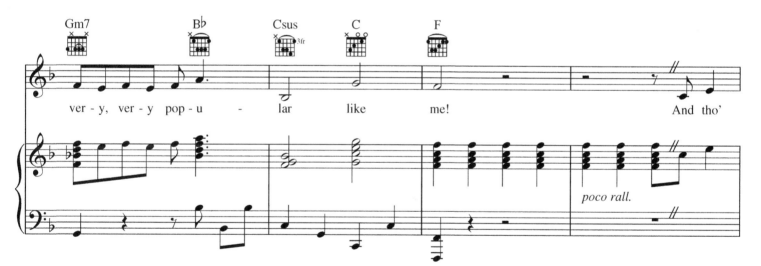

ver - y, ver - y pop - u - lar like me! And tho'

Freely

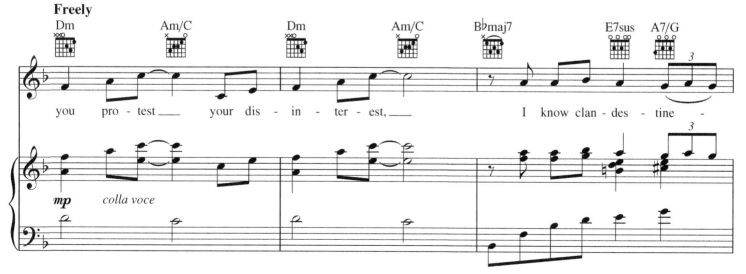

you pro - test __ your dis - in - ter - est, __ I know clan - des - tine -

ly You're gon - na grin and bear it your new - found pop - u - lar - it -

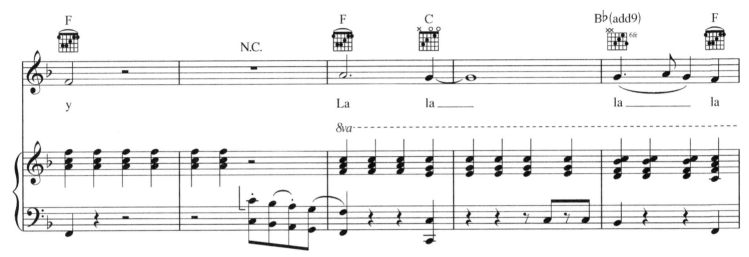

y La la _____ la _____ la

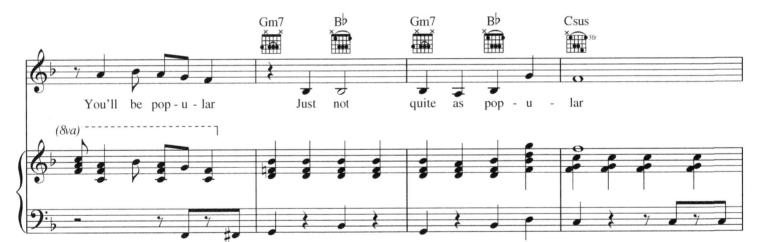

You'll be pop - u - lar Just not quite as pop - u - lar

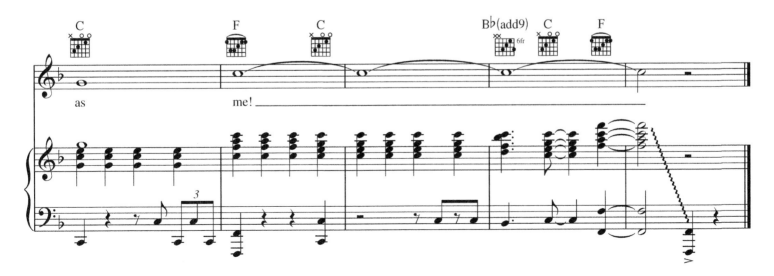

as me! _____

WHAT IS THIS FEELING?

Music and Lyrics by
STEPHEN SCHWARTZ

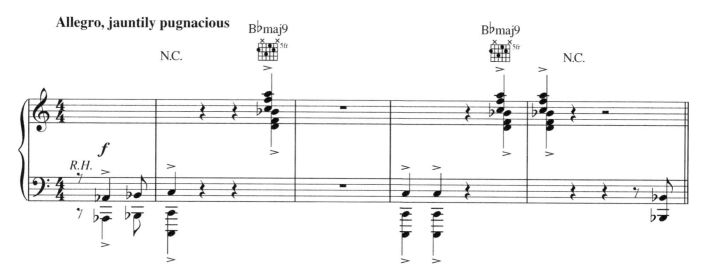

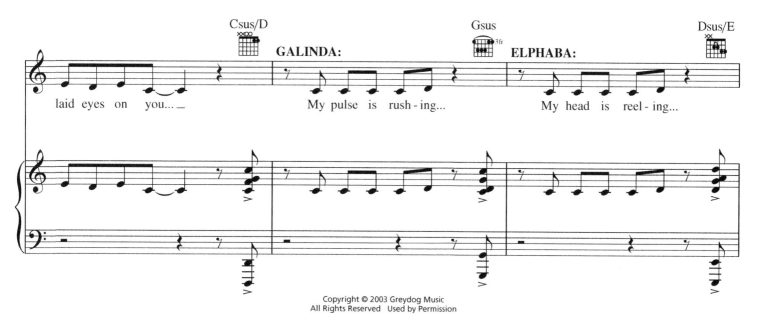

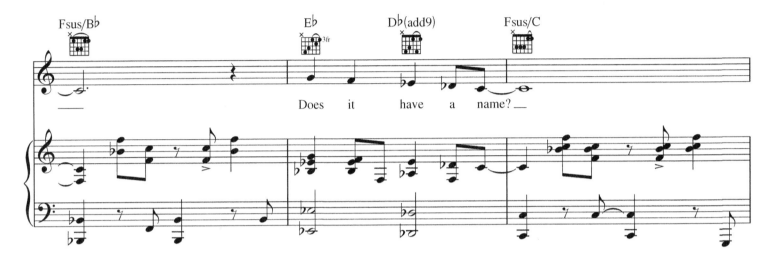

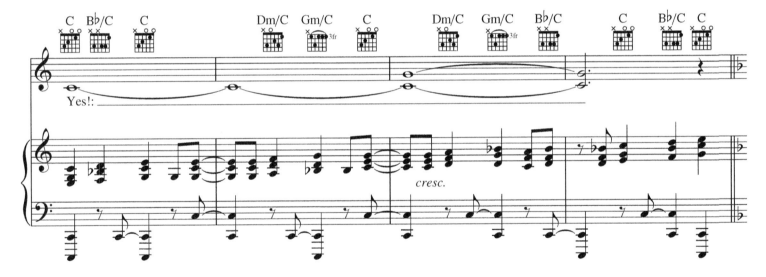

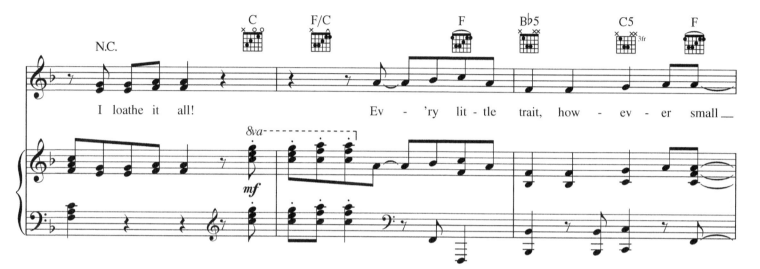

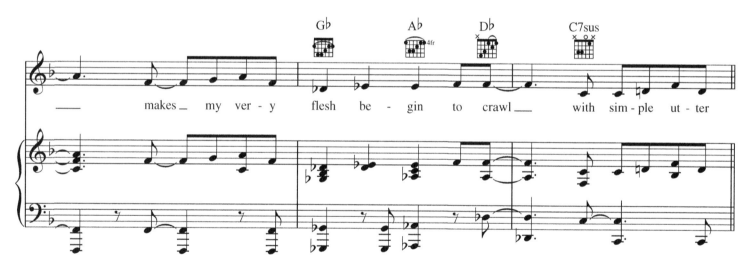

_____ such to-tal de-tes-ta-tion   It's so pure! _ So

strong! _____ Though _ I do ad-mit it came on fast, _

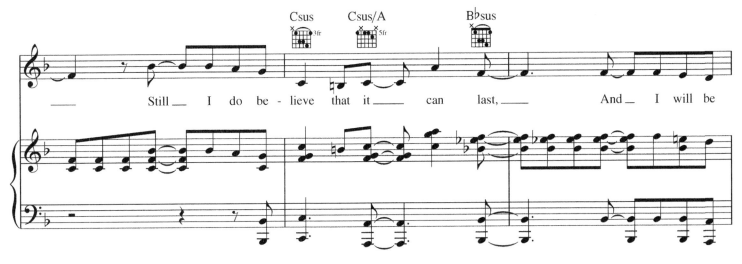

_____ Still _ I do be-lieve that it _ can last, _____ And _ I will be

loath-ing, _ loath-ing you my whole

what is this feel - ing?   Does   it   have   a   name?___

Ev - 'ry lit - tle trait how - ev - er small ___ makes ___ my ver - y

___   Yes...

flesh be - gin to crawl! ____

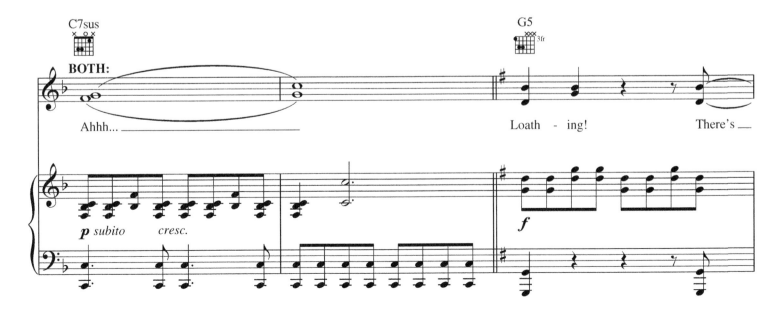

Ahhh... _____   Loath - ing!   There's ___

BOTH:

a strange ex-hil-a-ra-tion in ___ such to-tal de-tes-

ta-tion   So pure, ___ so strong! ___

Though ___ I do ad-mit it came on fast, ___ still, ___ I do be-

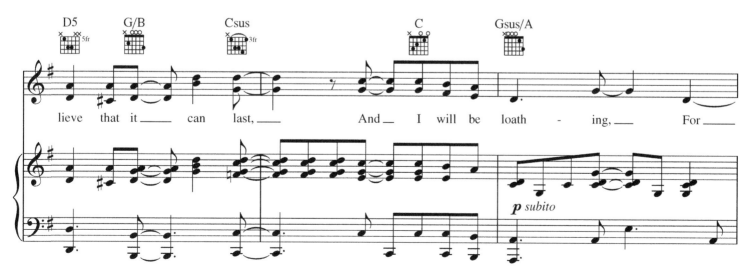

lieve that it ___ can last, ___ And ___ I will be loath-ing, ___ For ___

p *subito*

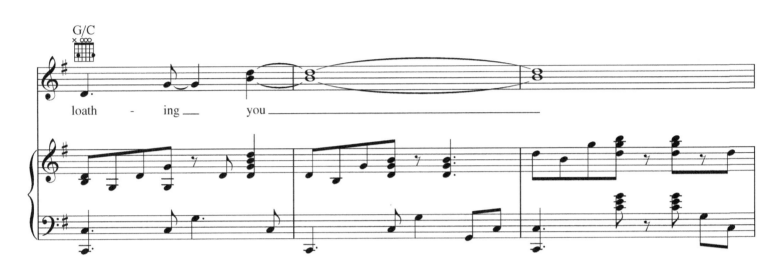

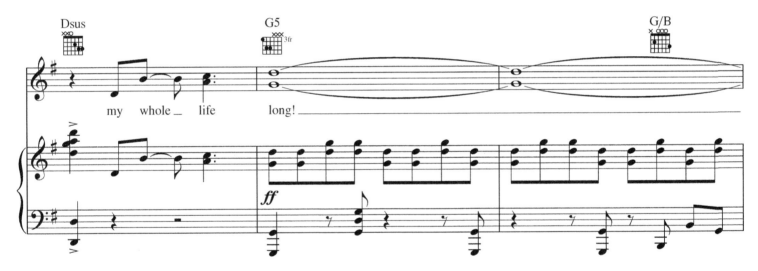

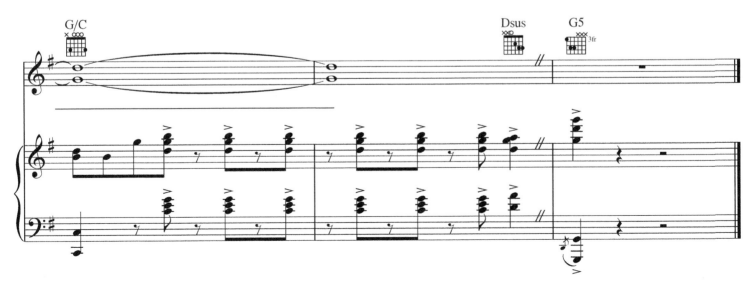

THE WIZARD AND I

Music and Lyrics by
STEPHEN SCHWARTZ

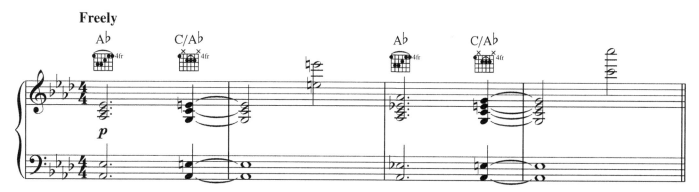

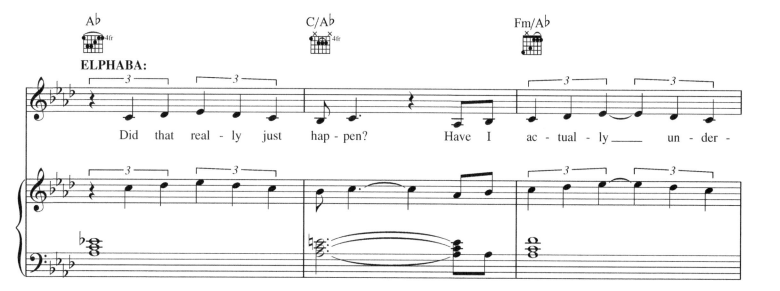

ELPHABA:
Did that real-ly just hap-pen? Have I ac-tual-ly ____ un-der-

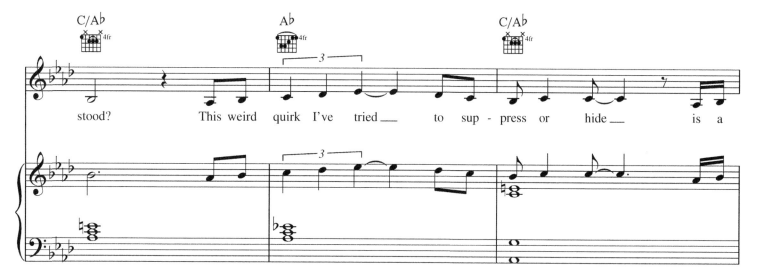

stood? This weird quirk I've tried ____ to sup-press or hide ____ is a

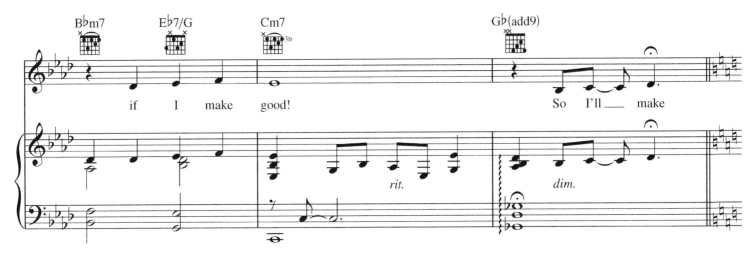

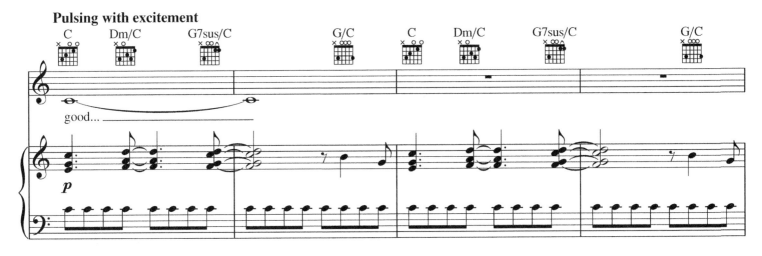

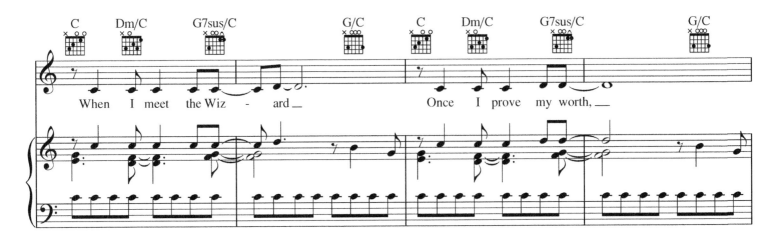

and then I meet the Wiz - ard ___ What I've wait - ed for ___ since—

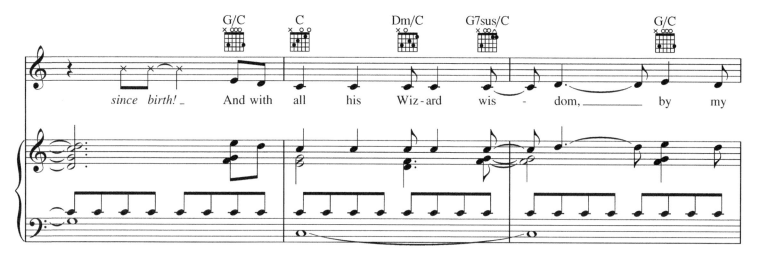

since birth! _ And with all his Wiz - ard wis - dom, _____ by my

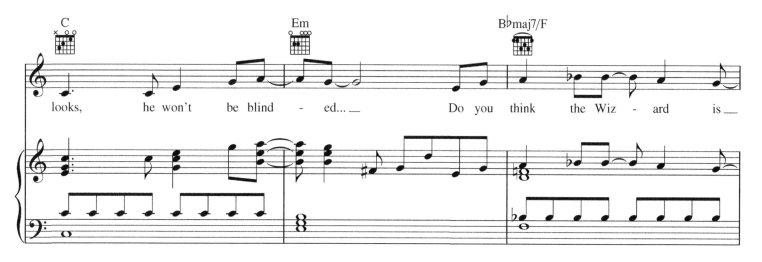

looks, he won't be blind - ed... ___ Do you think the Wiz - ard is ___

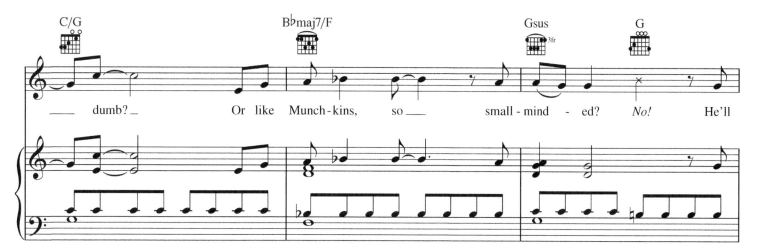

___ dumb? _ Or like Munch-kins, so ___ small - mind - ed? No! He'll

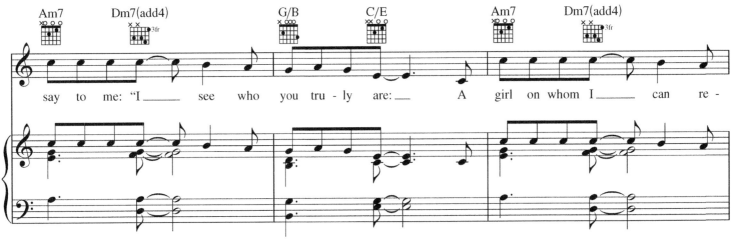

say to me: "I _____ see who you tru - ly are: ___ A girl on whom I _____ can re -

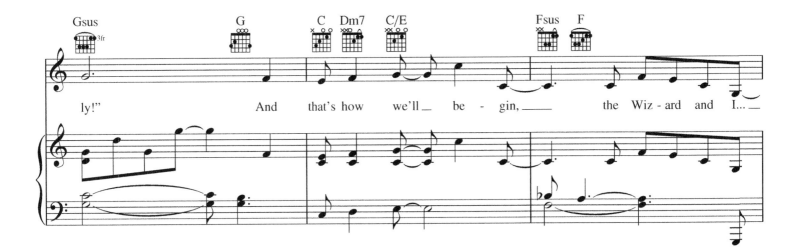

ly!" And that's how we'll _ be - gin, ____ the Wiz - ard and I... ___

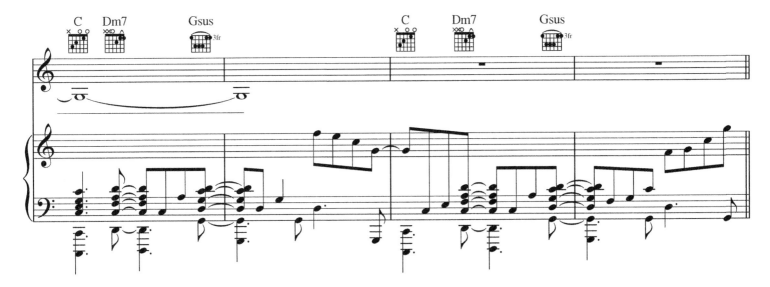

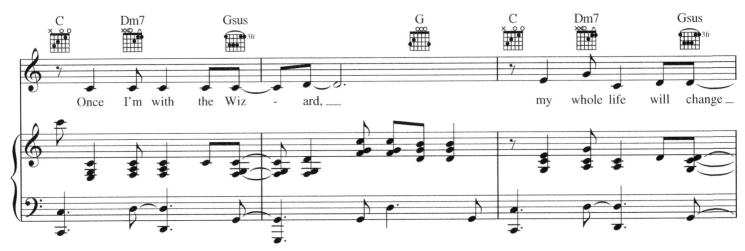

Once I'm with the Wiz - ard, ___ my whole life will change _

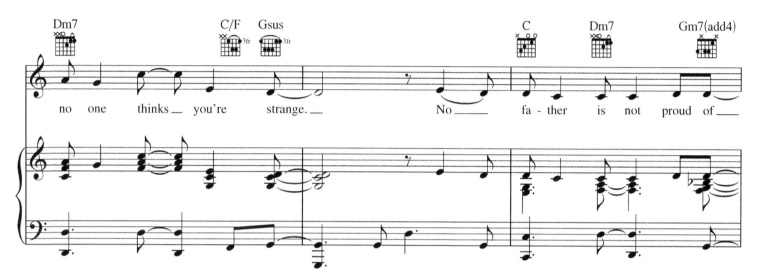

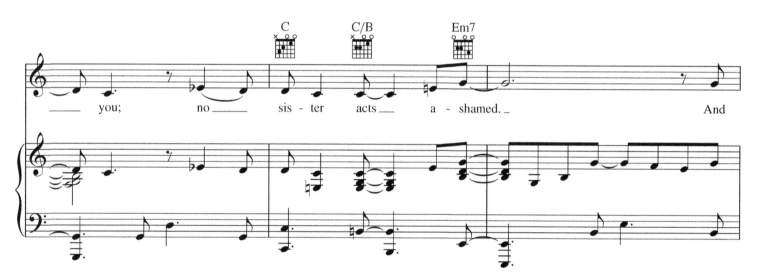

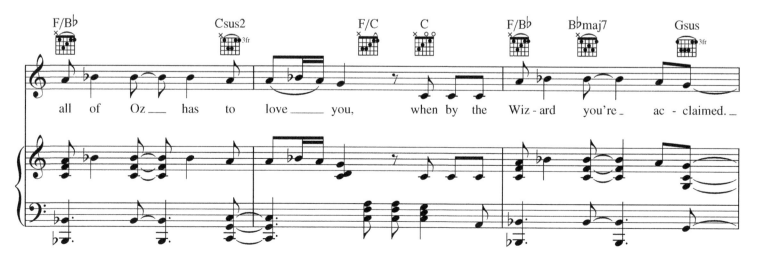

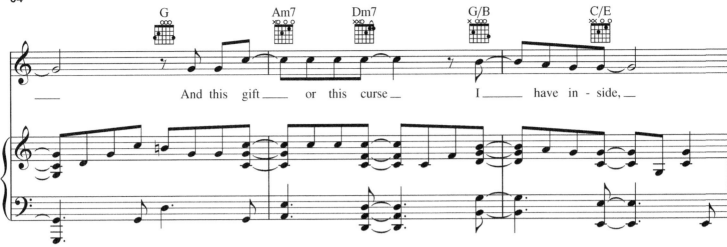

And this gift___ or this curse___ I___ have in - side,___

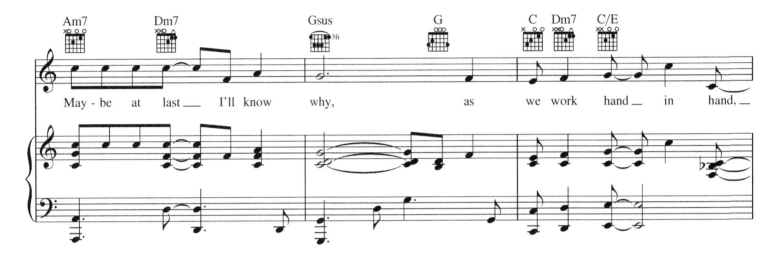

May - be at last___ I'll know why, as we work hand___ in hand,___

Più mosso

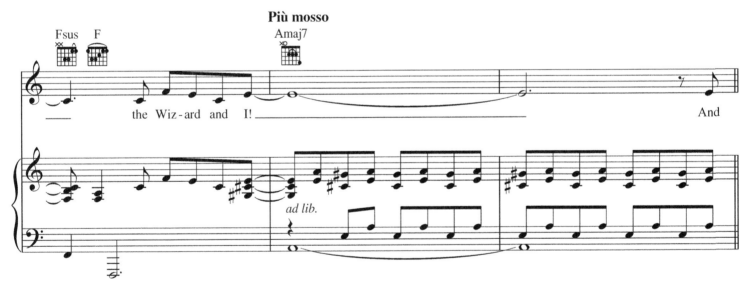

___ the Wiz - ard and I!_____ And

one day, he'll say to me: "El - pha - ba, A girl who is___ so su -

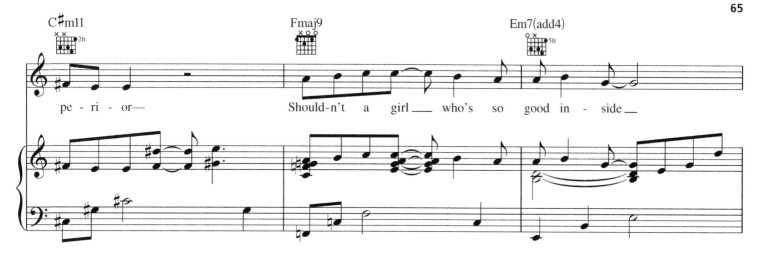

pe - ri - or— Should-n't a girl __ who's so good in - side __

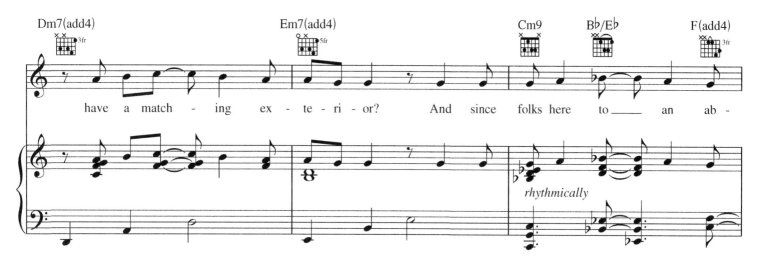

have a match - ing ex - te - ri - or? And since folks here to __ an ab -

rhythmically

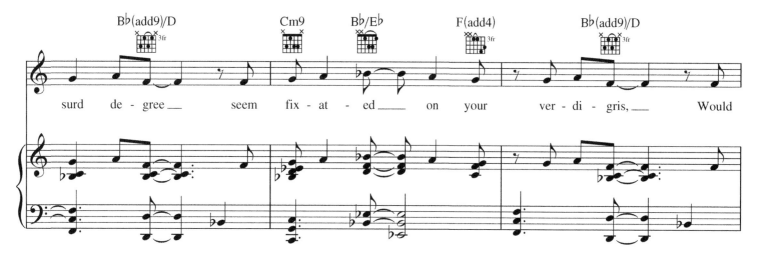

surd de - gree __ seem fix - at - ed __ on your ver - di - gris, __ Would

it be all __ right by __ you __ If I de - green - i - fy __

dim. e rit.

mp

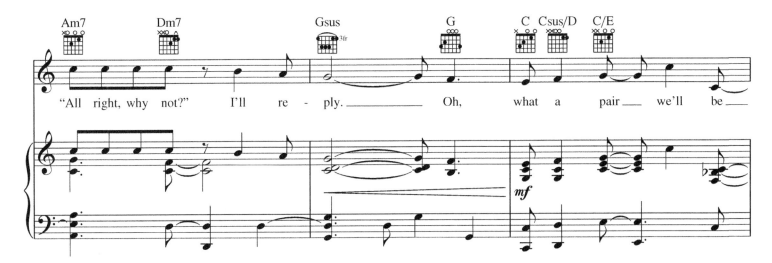

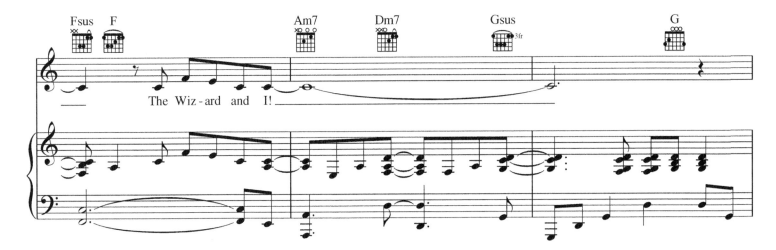

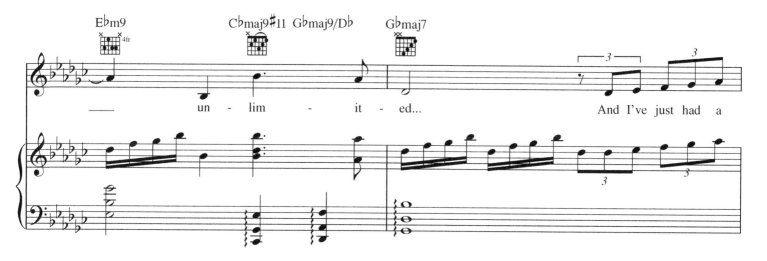

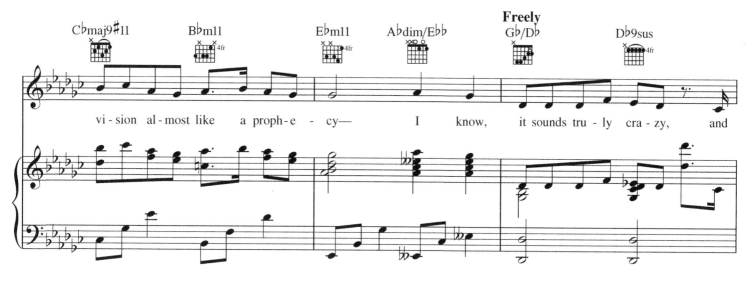

- ard, ___ feel - ing things I've nev - er felt, ___

accel.

And though I'd nev - er show ___ it, I'll be so hap - py, I ___ could melt! ___

poco a poco accel.

Bright, triumphant

And so it will be ___ for the rest of my life, ___ and I'll

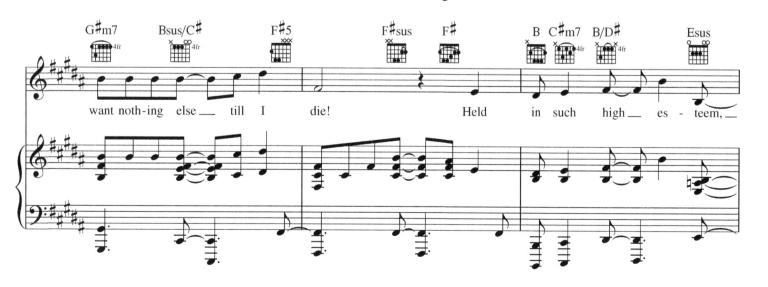

want noth-ing else ___ till I die! Held in such high ___ es - teem, ___

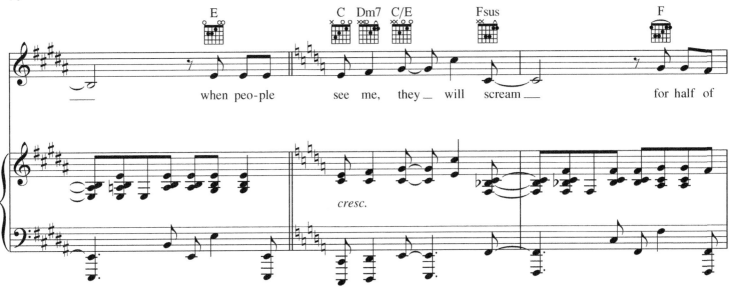

when peo-ple see me, they _ will scream _ for half of

Oz - 's fav - 'rite team: _____ The Wiz - ard and

A tempo

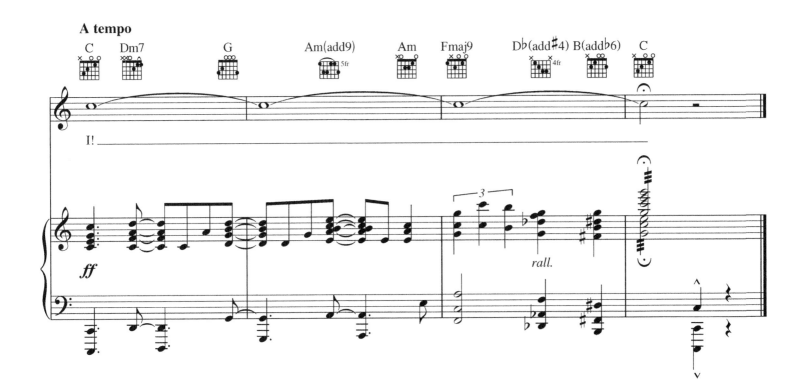

I! _____

THE ULTIMATE SONGBOOKS

HAL•LEONARD PIANO PLAY-ALONG

These great songbook/audio packs come with our standard arrangements for piano and voice with guitar chord frames plus audio. The audio includes a full performance of each song, as well as a second track without the piano part so you can play "lead" with the band!

BOOK/CD PACKS

1. **Movie Music** 00311072 .... $14.95
7. **Love Songs** 00311078 .... $14.95
12. **Christmas Favorites** 00311137 .... $15.95
15. **Favorite Standards** 00311146 .... $14.95
27. **Andrew Lloyd Webber Greats** 00311179 .... $14.95
28. **Lennon & McCartney** 00311180 .... $14.95
29. **The Beach Boys** 00311181 .... $14.95
31. **Carpenters** 00311183 .... $17.99
44. **Frank Sinatra – Popular Hits** 00311277 .... $14.95
45. **Frank Sinatra – Most Requested Songs**
    00311278 .... $14.95
53. **Grease** 00311450 .... $14.95
64. **God Bless America** 00311489 .... $14.95
71. **George Gershwin** 00102687 .... $24.99
72. **Van Morrison** 00103053 .... $14.99
77. **Elton John Favorites** 00311884 .... $14.99
78. **Eric Clapton** 00311885 .... $14.99
81. **Josh Groban** 00311901 .... $14.99
82. **Lionel Richie** 00311902 .... $14.99
86. **Barry Manilow** 00311935 .... $14.99
87. **Patsy Cline** 00311936 .... $14.99
90. **Irish Favorites** 00311969 .... $14.99
92. **Disney Favorites** 00311973 .... $14.99
97. **Great Classical Themes** 00312020 .... $14.99
98. **Christmas Cheer** 00312021 .... $14.99
103. **Gospel Favorites** 00312044 .... $14.99
105. **Bee Gees** 00312055 .... $14.99
106. **Carole King** 00312056 .... $14.99
107. **Bob Dylan** 00312057 .... $14.99
108. **Simon & Garfunkel** 00312058 .... $14.99
114. **Motown** 00312176 .... $14.99
115. **John Denver** 00312249 .... $14.99
123. **Chris Tomlin** 00312563 .... $14.99
125. **Katy Perry** 00109373 .... $14.99

BOOKS/ONLINE AUDIO

5. **Disney** 00311076 .... $14.99
8. **The Piano Guys – Uncharted** 00202549 .... $24.99
9. **The Piano Guys – Christmas Together**
   00259567 .... $24.99
16. **Coldplay** 00316506 .... $16.99
20. **La La Land** 00241591 .... $19.99
24. **Les Misérables** 00311169 .... $14.99
25. **The Sound of Music** 00311175 .... $15.99
30. **Elton John Hits** 00311182 .... $16.99
32. **Adele** 00156222 .... $24.99
33. **Peanuts™** 00311227 .... $14.99
34. **A Charlie Brown Christmas** 00311228 .... $16.99
46. **Wicked** 00311317 .... $16.99
62. **Billy Joel Hits** 00311465 .... $14.99
65. **Casting Crowns** 00311494 .... $14.99
69. **Pirates of the Caribbean** 00311807 .... $15.99
73. **Mamma Mia! – The Movie** 00311831 .... $15.99
76. **Pride & Prejudice** 00311862 .... $15.99
83. **Phantom of the Opera** 00311903 .... $15.99
113. **Queen** 00312164 .... $16.99
117. **Alicia Keys** 00312306 .... $17.99
118. **Adele** 00312307 .... $14.99
126. **Bruno Mars** 00123121 .... $14.99
127. **Star Wars** 00110282 .... $14.99
128. **Frozen** 00126480 .... $16.99
130. **West Side Story** 00130738 .... $14.99
131. **The Piano Guys – Wonders**
     00141503 (Contains backing tracks only) $24.99

HAL•LEONARD®

7777 W. BLUEMOUND RD. P.O. BOX 13819 MILWAUKEE, WI 53213

Order online from your favorite music retailer at
halleonard.com

Prices, contents and availability subject to change without notice

0820
276